THE LOVE WE HAD
STAYS ON MY MIND

DR.CAROLYN BROWN

The Love We Had
Stays on My Mind

TABLE OF CONTENTS

DEDICATION

To my wonderful children, Carol, Allen, and Todd, your love and support have been a constant source of strength, and I am blessed to call you my own.

In Loving Memory of My Dear Husband, Elijah

Without your gentle and loving prodding, this book would not exist. Your constant encouragement continues to inspire me every day, and your love will forever remain in my heart. Though you are no longer with me, your presence is felt in every word of this work. I will always cherish the beautiful bond we shared, and your memory will live on in my soul.

FOREWORD
BY REV.ALLEN BROWN

I just finished reading my mother's book, *The Love We Had Stays on My Mind*, and I am honored to write the foreword for this beautiful love story. My name is Allen Brown, and I am my mother's second child and firstborn son. This is my first time writing a foreword, and I could not ask for a more meaningful story to introduce.

First and foremost, this book is a remarkable love story—a vivid testament to the deep bond my parents shared during their 41-year marriage. My parents were married in 1973, and tragically, in 2002, my father was diagnosed with a rare bone cancer. That was 29 years of love and life before their relationship faced one of its greatest challenges. While I lived through this difficult chapter, reading my mother's words has revealed so much more about the resilience and strength my father displayed in his fight, as well as the unwavering love and comfort my mother provided throughout his journey.

This book is truly amazing because it paints a vivid picture of what it means to love someone through sickness and health, through good and bad, and even through the parting brought by death. My parents' love has been a blueprint for my own marriage. I've been blessed to share

27 years with my wife, Melissa, and I know that who they were and how they loved each other helped shaped me into the man I am today in life and in my own marriage.

As you read this memoir, you'll see that it is more than a story—it's a testament. Whether you are currently in a marriage, navigating grief after the loss of a loved one, or facing an entirely different challenge in life, this book offers comfort, inspiration, and hope. My mother, Dr. Carolyn Brown, has written a story that will resonate deeply, drawing strength from her faith in God and the enduring love she and my father shared.

Although this is my mother's story, I know I'm not being biased when I say it is an amazing read. It's a powerful example of what true love looks like and how it can transcend even the hardest moments of life. I am honored to present this foreword and pray that every word of this story transforms and uplifts you as much as it did for me.

Mommy, I love you. Dad, thank you for being an incredible example and setting the tone for what love should look like in a relationship. I love you both.

Your son,
Allen

INTRODUCTION
IN THE ECHOES OF LOVE

As I reflect on the journey of our love, the memories linger in my mind like a sweet melody. Our story is etched in the tapestry of time, a narrative of joy, challenges, and enduring affection. Join me in revisiting the moments that define the essence of the love we shared—a love that remains vivid and timeless in the corridors of my thoughts.

In the quiet corners of my heart, where memories linger and love resides, there exists a story that begs to be told. This is not a tale of goodbyes; it is a celebration of a love so profound that even in loss, its essence dances through the corridors of my soul.

His name was Elijah, and this book is a tribute to the man who painted my world with hues of joy, laughter, and shared dreams. As I pen down the pages of our journey, I invite you to step into the sanctuary of our love, a love that refuses to be confined by the boundaries of time.

"The Love We Had Stays On My Mind" is more than a recounting of days and nights; it is an exploration of the enduring power of love, the kind that transcends the physical realm. In these words, I hope to capture the essence of a life well-lived, a love deeply cherished, and the strength discovered in the aftermath of farewell. I cannot begin this without first acknowledging the quiet strength Elijah brought to every moment of our lives. His presence had a way of anchoring the storms, bringing peace when the world seemed chaotic.

I remember the way he would look at me, not just with his eyes but with his heart, as if in every glance, he was telling me that I was his world. That kind of love, that unwavering devotion, has a way of settling into your bones, making you feel invincible. Even now, as I sit in the stillness of these days without him, I feel his love as strongly as I did when he was right beside me.

One of the most beautiful aspects of our relationship was how Elijah was never afraid to show his love. He would walk into a room and light it up, not with grand gestures, but with the small, thoughtful things that made every day extraordinary. The way he brewed my tea just right, even on those mornings when he was running late. The way he'd sit and listen, really listen, to my worries, my dreams, my thoughts. These small acts, though they might seem insignificant to the outside world, wove together the fabric of our lives.

There was something magical about the way we lived in the ordinary moments—because, with Elijah, nothing was truly ordinary. He had this way of making me feel like we were the only two people in the world when we were together. He saw me, not just the version of myself I showed the world, but the deeper parts of me, the parts that I sometimes tried to hide. He embraced all of it, loving me without hesitation or condition.

As I embark on this writing journey, I am guided by the whispers of shared laughter, the warmth of intertwined hands, and the lingering scent of his favorite cologne. His love was a quiet symphony that played softly in the background of my life, but now, in the silence of his absence, I find myself listening more closely, cherishing the melody he left behind.

This book is not just about grief; it is about the unwavering light that continues to glow even in the shadows of loss. It is about finding strength in the love we shared and the comfort in knowing that love doesn't end—it transforms. It evolves, becoming something different but no less powerful.

I can still feel his presence, particularly in the quiet moments—when the house is still, and the only sound is the soft rustle of the wind outside. It is in those moments that I hear him most clearly, not in words but in the feeling, the quiet reassurance that he is still with me, watching over me, loving me as fiercely as ever.

So, join me as we navigate through the tapestry of our love story—a story that began with a glance, unfolded through shared dreams, and now, eternally resides in the love we had, the love that stays on my mind.

This is my tribute, my memoir, and a testament to a love that remains, even when the physical presence is but a memory. Elijah is not gone; he is simply elsewhere, and the love we shared continues to guide me, to uplift me, and to remind me that some connections are so deep, they transcend the boundaries of this world.

In the echoes of love, I find my peace, my strength, and my reason for continuing. I walk forward, not alone, but with Elijah by my side, his love wrapped around me like a warm blanket on a cold winter's night.

The chapters ahead will reflect this journey—the love, the loss, and most importantly, the life that continues, filled with the beautiful memories we created. This is not just my story; it is ours, and I hope it will resonate with anyone who has ever loved and lost, and yet, found solace in the knowledge that love, true love, never truly leaves.

CHAPTER 1
THE GENTLEMAN I COULDN'T RESIST

In the bustling corridors of our workplace, destiny silently wove the threads that would bind our lives together. Elijah, my husband, had been a fixture in that professional landscape long before my arrival. From the very beginning, he stood out—a gentleman in the truest sense of the word.

Our initial interactions were the simple exchanges of colleagues. A polite "hello, how are you?" and the typical small talk that permeates workplace conversations. Yet, from those seemingly ordinary moments, an extraordinary connection quietly flourishes...

Elijah's demeanor exuded warmth that reached beyond the confines of professional courtesy. There was an unspoken kindness in his eyes, a gentleness that drew me in. I couldn't put my finger on it at the time, but something whispered that this man would play a significant role in my life. I kept my distance initially, navigating the professional landscape. Yet, fate seemed to have other plans for us.

In the serendipity of our workplace, every conference meeting became an opportunity for our paths to intertwine, leading us to occupy adjacent seats. The cafeteria, a place of shared meals, mirrored our connection as we stood in line, either behind or in front of each other. Even the morning train, an everyday routine, transformed into a daily rendezvous as Elijah boarded the same car I occupied.

As these encounters multiplied, I couldn't help but wonder – were these mere incidents or part of a grand design? Was it the universe orchestrating our meetings, or perhaps, a touch of divine intervention?

In the echoes of love that unfolded between us, I began to believe that our story was genuinely woven by a force greater than chance, a tale scripted by destiny itself. And so, as we embarked on this journey, I couldn't help but feel that Elijah and I were meant to be together, guided by the invisible threads of fate.

As days turned into weeks and weeks into months, our exchanges grew from mere pleasantries to genuine conversations. I learned about books he read , his love for jazz music, and the subtle variations of his character that endeared him to all who knew him. However, I remained uncertain about the depths of his feelings, as emotions often hide behind the mask of professionalism.

Then came the day when the unexpected script of my life unfolded. Elijah, with a sincerity that resonated in his eyes, asked me out. The excitement that bubbled within me was evident, rendering me momentarily speechless. In that moment, I saw a glimpse of our future, and it was a future I eagerly embraced. He asked me for my phone number, stating he would call me Saturday morning, letting me know what time he would pick me up.

However, amidst all the joy and excitement, there was a moment of disappointment. I vividly remember the anticipation I felt when Elijah asked for my phone number. My heart raced with excitement as I eagerly scribbled it down, but in my haste, I made a mistake. Saturday morning, I waited by the phone, my heart fluttering with every passing minute, but the call never came. All weekend, I held onto the hope that maybe he had just been busy, but deep down, I knew something was wrong.

As the weekend passed without any word from Elijah, I couldn't shake the feeling of disappointment and regret. I wished I could go back and double-check the number I had given him, to ensure that he had the correct one.

But despite the setback, I refused to let it dampen my spirit and would wait to see what he would have to say about not calling me.

When I saw Elijah on Monday to inquire why he hadn't called over the weekend, he gently explained that he hadn't been able to reach me because I had given him the wrong number. In my hurry to give him my contact information, I had inadvertently written down the last digit incorrectly.

Realizing my mistake, a mix of embarrassment and relief washed over me. We laughed it off together, deciding to give it another try. The following weekend, all went well. From that moment on, we were a couple, our hearts aligned in a newfound harmony that seemed to echo the beauty of our shared experiences and the resilience of our love.

As we continued to journey through life's twists and turns, I held onto the belief that sometimes, the greatest adventures begin with a wrong number and a second chance.

Our courtship was a dance of discovery, each step revealing more about the person who would become my life partner. Within the span of ten months, we found ourselves standing at the altar, surrounded by the promise of forever.

On, reminiscing about the day Elijah asked me to marry him brings back such wonderful memories. We were in New York City for a weekend, and little did I know he had planned the entire trip with a surprise proposal in mind.

The first day, we had a delightful lunch at Sylvia's, and afterwards, to my surprise, there was a horse and buggy ride through Central Park. Elijah had remembered how I once mentioned how much I'd love a ride through Central Park in a horse-drawn carriage, finding it incredibly romantic.

Next, we walked through the beautiful Central-Park-Conservatory-Garden. Memories flooded my mind because we had visited this spot previously during a business trip, where we witnessed a couple's heartfelt proposal. Recalling that moment, tears welled up in my eyes, perhaps even more than they did for the bride-to-be back then. I had shared with Elijah how I found it to be the most beautiful and romantic location for a proposal, and to my surprise, he remembered.

Stepping into the garden, surrounded by the most beautiful flowers, Elijah took my hand and in the center of it all went down on one knee, a beautiful little box in hand. As he looked up at me, he said, "Carolyn, with you, I have found everything I need to have a wonderful and glorious life. Will you marry me?" For a moment, I was speechless, overwhelmed with love for this incredible man. Without hesitation, I finally managed to say, "Yes, I will marry you." It was a moment filled with joy, love, and the promise of a beautiful future together.

It was such a magical moment, and I'll forever cherish how thoughtful and unforgettable he made that day.

God blessed our union with three beautiful children, gifts that brought immeasurable joy into our lives. Our home echoed with laughter, and our hearts swelled with the love that defined our family.

Yet, as life often unfolds its unpredictable narrative, a shadow casts itself upon our idyllic existence. Elijah, the pillar of strength in our family, fell ill. The joy that once permeated our days faced an unexpected adversary. In the face of adversity, our love would be tested, and the strength of our bond would be revealed in the test of uncertainty.

This is the story of our love—a journey marked by the gentle beginnings of workplace encounters, the whirlwind romance, and the challenges that awaited us on the horizon. As I recount these memories, I am reminded that even in the face of illness, love has the power to endure and illuminate the darkest corners of our lives.

CHAPTER 2
UNRAVELING MYSTERY

The morning routine became a constant ritual, a canvas painted with love and routine. As Elijah dressed for work, he adorned himself with an effortless handsomeness that never failed to capture my heart. A quick kiss exchanged, and the words "Have a good day, honey" lingered in the air as he ventured into the world. I often found myself at the window, a silent observer, watching him stride purposefully to catch the train into the city.

In those moments, I marveled at the gift of this man in my life. It seemed as though God had crafted him with a special touch, tailor-made to complement the contours of my soul. The love that enveloped us was genuine, a connection that transcended the ordinary. I had no doubt—this man was my destiny.

The love we shared was a reflection of a divine design, a sentiment mirrored in the words penned by the Apostle Paul in the Bible. Ephesians 5:25-28, echoed the essence of Elijah's love for me:

"Husbands, love your wives, even as Christ also loved the church, and gave himself for it; that he might sanctify and cleanse it with the washing of water by the word,

That he might present it to himself a glorious church, not having spot, or wrinkle, or any such thing; but that it should be holy and without blemish.

So ought men to love their wives as their own bodies. He that loveth his wife loveth himself."

In the reflection of these words, I saw Elijah's love as a selfless devotion, a commitment to my well-being and spiritual growth. Just as Christ's love for the church was pure and sacrificial, Elijah's love mirrored that divine essence. Our shared journey became a testament to the enduring power of love, guided by the wisdom found in ancient scriptures. And so, as we embraced the teachings of Ephesians, our love story unfolded as a beautiful chapter in the grand narrative of a love designed by something greater than ourselves.

In the quiet moments over a cup of tea, I would offer a silent prayer of gratitude. "Thank You, Lord," I whispered, acknowledging the blessing of a love that mirrored the selfless devotion described in those sacred verses.

Yet, as the days unfolded, 29 years of us together was about to change as an unwelcome visitor cast its shadow upon our haven of love in 2002. Elijah, my beacon of strength, began to falter. The vibrant mornings transformed into a series of doctor visits, tests, and unanswered questions. We found ourselves on an unexpected journey, facing a mystery that eluded even the most skilled physicians.

In the face of uncertainty, our love became the anchor that steadied us. As I sipped my tea, I clung to the memories of those mornings, the echoes of love, and the verses that spoke of a husband's sacrificial love. Little did we know that these verses would become a source of strength as we navigated the unknown path that lay ahead?

The vibrant spirit that once defined the essence of my husband now battles against an unseen force, manifesting in weariness and a struggle to walk.

I witness the unwavering commitment of a partner determined to unravel the mystery behind this unexpected transformation. Plans of idyllic vacations are momentarily set aside as the quest for answers takes precedence. The decision to seek the counsel of a recommended doctor becomes the pivotal moment, marking the beginning of a journey into the unknown realms of health and resilience.

Elijah and I found ourselves at a crossroads, grappling with unforeseen challenges that tested the very fabric of our connection. The resilience required in the face of unexpected twists became evident as we embarked on a journey into uncharted territory.

In the midst of this unpredictable terrain, our relationship encountered its first major test. The strength derived from facing adversity together became the anchor that held us steady. The vibrant spirit that once defined us now confronted shadows, and the decisions made in these moments would shape the course of our narrative.

Before we went to the doctor recommended, I found solace in prayer. Over the years of our marriage, one thing I have come to learn is that prayer is not the last resort—it's the first line of defense against any attack. So, I prayed.

Heavenly Father,

As I sit here with a heart heavy with concern for my beloved husband, I lift him up to you. I am asking for your divine touch to restore his health and ease his pain.

You, Lord, are the ultimate healer, and in this moment, I trust in your power to bring him comfort and healing. I plead for relief from any discomfort or ailment he is facing. Please, ease his pain, both physically and emotionally. Wrap him in your love and peace, granting him restful and rejuvenating sleep each night.

Lord, watch over him, guide his path toward wellness. May your presence be his source of strength, reminding him that he is not alone in this journey toward healing?

I believe in your mercy and grace to bring forth restoration and renewed health. In your name, I offer this prayer, placing my faith in your loving care.

Amen.

Sitting across from Dr. Goblieb, the doctor recommended, Elijah and I shared a moment of mutual support, our hands tightly clasped. Dr. Goblieb, a warm and approachable figure, had left a positive impression during our phone conversation when I made the appointment.

As we became acquainted in person, Dr. Goblieb turned his attention to Elijah, encouraging him to share the details of what he was experiencing. Elijah began to list his symptoms: nausea, loss of appetite, weakness, hip pain, fatigue, frequent urination, and unquenchable thirst. I listened, realizing there were aspects of his condition he had not disclosed to me.

Taking immediate action, Dr. Goblieb called for the nurse to assist Elijah to the examination room. There, the thorough examination, and blood work commenced. A necessary step in uncovering the root of Elijah's health challenges. Dr. Goblieb assured us that he would contact us once the results were back from the lab.

As we walked into our house the air in the room held a mix of anticipation and concern as we awaited answers that would shed light on the mysterious symptoms Elijah was facing. The journey toward understanding and healing had begun, and with each passing moment, we clung to the hope that the medical investigation would provide the clarity we so desperately sought.

CHAPTER 3
A SHATTERED REALITY

The following week brought with it both anticipation and anxiety as Dr. Goblieb's call summoned us to his office. With hope in our hearts, we yearned for answers, a diagnosis that could be treated, and a return to the normalcy we once knew.

As we stepped into the doctor's office, an unspoken heaviness seemed to settle around us. Dr. Goblieb gestured for us to take a seat, and as he retrieved a folder, a sense of foreboding gripped me. His hesitation as he began to speak only deepened my unease. "Mr. Brown, we received your blood work back, and I..." he paused, the weight of his next words palpable in the air. "I am sorry; you have a form of cancer called Multiple Myeloma."

Elijah and I exchanged disbelieving glances. The term was foreign to us, and its implications hung heavy in the room. Dr. Goblieb continued to explain the gravity of the diagnosis, the challenges that lay ahead, and the necessary steps for treatment.

In that moment, our reality shattered. The hope for a simple solution evaporated; replaced by the daunting realization that we were facing an adversary we had never anticipated. Multiple Myeloma—an unfamiliar name that now held the power to redefine our lives.

As we grappled with the shock and disbelief, a new chapter unfolded—one marked by the uncertain path of navigating through the complexities of cancer, resilience, and the unwavering bond that would be tested in the face of this unforeseen challenge.

As we left the doctor's office, a heavy silence enveloped us, both uncertain of what to say or how to react to the news. In that moment, Elijah reached out and gently took my hand. He looked at me with a reassuring gaze and said, "I don't want you to worry. I will get through this." I squeezed his hand tightly and replied, "No, we will get through this together."

In our shared journey, the term "Multiple Myeloma" was a stranger to both of us. The doctor had provided some initial information, and we were armed with pamphlets, yet it felt like stepping into the abyss of the unknown. Post-dinner, driven by a blend of curiosity and a yearning to comprehend this unexpected intrusion into our lives, I turned to my computer.

Embarking on an earnest search for information about Multiple Myeloma, my fingers danced across the keyboard, hoping to unravel its intricacies, treatment options, and the potential landscape of our future. As I typed, the computer unveiled that Multiple Myeloma is a type of cancer originating in plasma cells—a variety of white blood cells. These cells, normally responsible for producing antibodies to combat infections, in the case of multiple myeloma, turn cancerous, multiplying uncontrollably and overshadowing the production of healthy blood cells in the bone marrow.

Some key revelations from my digital exploration were:

Bone Marrow and Bone Damage: The excessive growth of these plasma cells can lead to bone marrow overcrowding and inflict damage on bones, causing pain and potential fractures.

Symptoms: The computer relayed common symptoms, including bone pain (especially in the back and hips), fatigue, weakness, frequent infections, unexplained weight loss, and kidney problems.

Diagnosis: The process of diagnosis typically involves blood tests, bone marrow biopsy, imaging studies (such as X-rays or MRI), and other laboratory tests to gauge the extent of the disease.

Staging: Understanding that multiple myeloma is staged based on the extent of the disease, which aids in determining the appropriate treatment approach.

Treatment: Various treatment options were outlined, ranging from chemotherapy and immunomodulatory drugs to proteasome inhibitors, stem cell transplantation, and targeted therapies. The choice of treatment is contingent on factors such as the patient's overall health and the stage of the disease.

Life Expectancy: I learned that life expectancy in multiple myeloma can vary widely based on factors like the stage at diagnosis, overall health, response to treatment, and specific characteristics of the cancer.

This dive into the realm of medical knowledge became my coping mechanism, a way to empower myself with understanding, and to stand as a supportive partner for Elijah. Little did we realize that this exploration would evolve into an indispensable part of our shared experience, helping us face the challenges that lay ahead.

After much information from medical professionals and exploring the internet, it was time to tell our children.

We had three grown children. How would we tell them their father had cancer? They needed to know what was going on concerning their father's health. We knew they would be just as concerned as we were and ask questions.

The weight of the unspoken truth hung heavy as we coped with the daunting task of informing our three grown children Carol, Allen, and Todd about their father's battle with cancer. The need for transparency and the realization that they deserved to be brought into the fold of our shared experience became undeniable.

The challenge was not just conveying the diagnosis but finding the right words to articulate the gravity of the situation without causing unnecessary alarm. We recognized that they would harbor concerns and pose questions that mirrored our own anxieties.

As we gathered our children, the room echoed with a mix of emotions — apprehension, vulnerability, and the unspoken strength that comes from facing adversity as a united front. The conversation unfolded, navigating through the complexities of medical terminology and the raw reality of their father's health journey.

In those moments, honesty became our compass, guiding us through the difficult terrain of conveying painful news. We shared the diagnosis, the treatment plan, and the uncertainties that lay ahead. Their reactions were a mixture of concern, love, and a shared determination to stand by their father's side.

Carol was the first to speak. Taking a deep breath as she rushed over to him; "Daddy, I can't believe this. This news is breaking my heart. You've always been my hero, my pillar of strength, and the thought of you facing something like this is just... it's overwhelming."

"Daddy, I love you so much. We're in this together. You've been there for me always, and now it's our turn to be there for you. We'll face whatever comes our way as a family, with love and resilience. No matter what lies ahead, our family bond is unbreakable. Dad, we'll navigate this journey together, and I'll be right by your side every step of the way."

Allen walked over to his father saying, "Dad, hearing this news is a lot to process, but I want you to know that our faith will guide us through this challenging time. I believe in the power of prayer and the strength that comes from leaning on our spiritual foundation."

"As a pastor, I've witnessed the resilience that faith can instill in people facing adversity. We'll gather as a family and pray for your healing. God has seen us through difficult times before, and I trust that He will provide the strength we need for this journey."

"Dad, you've been a source of inspiration for so many, and now, it's our turn to rally around you. We'll hold on to hope, and I'll be here to offer not just my prayers but also any support you need. Our faith will be our anchor, and together, as a family and a community, we'll face this with courage and unwavering trust in God's plan."

Todd for a moment sat quietly with his head down. "Dad, I... I don't even know what to say. This is a lot to take in, and it feels like everything just turned upside down. You've always been there for us, and the thought of you going through this is tough. My voice may be trembling, but please know it's not out of fear; it's out of concern and love. We're a family, and we stick together through thick and thin. Whatever it takes, whatever the road ahead looks like, I'm with you every step of the way."

"And Dad, if there's anything I can do to help or support you, just say the word. We've got your back, always. Let's face this head-on, as a family, and show whatever this thing is that it picked the wrong family to mess with. We're fighters, and we'll get through this together."

There was a collective understanding in the room, an unspoken agreement that we were in this together. The uncertainty of the journey ahead lingered, but in that moment, I found strength in the unity of our family. We would face this adversity as a team.

Telling our children about their father's cancer was not just an announcement; it was an invitation for them to join us in this collective journey of resilience, support, and unwavering family unity. The gravity of the moment was met with open hearts, an unspoken pact to face the challenges together, and a shared commitment to navigate the unknown with strength, love, and the enduring bond that defines family.

CHAPTER 4
NAVIGATING TREATMENT CROSSROADS

In our discussion with Dr. Goblieb before Elijah embarked on his initial treatment, we found ourselves faced with a decision regarding the method of administering the medication—needles or a vein-access device.

Elijah opted for the vein-access device.

Dr. Goblieb took the time to clarify that the primary benefit of opting for the vein-access device lies in the direct delivery of chemotherapy medications into the port, bypassing the need for repeated needle sticks. It became evident that many individuals undergoing chemotherapy opt for a port implantation when it is recommended by their treatment team. This choice offered us a clearer understanding of the options available, and the considerations involved in Elijah's treatment journey.

He explained that Elijah needed a port for chemotherapy and medication administration. The port is a discreet, subcutaneously implanted tube with a reservoir on the chest, allowing direct access to the bloodstream. Its durability allows for long-term use. He stressed the importance of meticulous care, including regular flushing, to maintain its functionality.

Elijah's port was accessed with a specialized needle for procedures, and when no longer needed, removal could be performed through a minor surgical procedure.

In essence, Elijah's journey involved the placement of a durable port for streamlined medical interventions, emphasizing the significance of attentive care and regular maintenance.

We were informed that the port Elijah had was a Subclavian line, placed in a vein behind the collarbone. However, after three weeks of the implant, Elijah's health took a drastic turn. He experienced symptoms such as fever, shaking chills, a racing heartbeat, confusion, changes in behavior, and a skin rash.

In response to his deteriorating condition, he was promptly taken to the emergency room and subsequently admitted to the hospital. Elijah's weakened immune system compounded the severity of his illness, necessitating his placement in the intensive care unit (ICU).

Understanding the gravity of the situation, the medical team-initiated treatment tailored to the type of central line in place, the severity of the infection, and Elijah's overall health. The unfolding events highlighted the complexities and challenges associated with managing complications arising from medical interventions.

We were informed that Elijah's port had to be removed, necessitating a shift to chemo infusions as the next step in his treatment. The medical team explained that infusion therapy involves delivering medications in liquid form directly into the body over time.

They outlined that the frequency and duration of Elijah's chemo treatments would depend on several factors, including the type of cancer he had, treatment objectives, the specific drugs used, and his body's response to the treatment. Typically, chemotherapy is administered in cycles, with periods of treatment followed by breaks to allow for recovery.

For Elijah, this might mean receiving chemo for a certain number of days or weeks, followed by a period of rest before starting the next cycle. The length of treatment and the number of cycles planned would be determined by his cancer care team.

In terms of how the drugs are metabolized and eliminated from the body, we were informed that most chemotherapy drugs are broken down by the kidneys and liver. Eventually, they are excreted from the body through urine or stool. The duration of drug elimination can vary based on factors such as the specific chemotherapy agents used, concurrent medications, age, and the overall function of Elijah's kidneys and liver.

The medical team assured us that they would provide guidance on any special precautions needed during Elijah's treatment to ensure his safety and well-being.

After Elijah's hospitalization for three weeks, he seemed to be on the road to recovery as his chemotherapy infusion began. However, his battle with Multiple Myeloma, a cancer of the bone, proved to be challenging. Despite our hopes, Elijah started experiencing balance issues, which deeply concerned me. From that moment on, I became Elijah's constant companion, ensuring he had the support he needed wherever he went.

As Elijah's health journey continued, he faced another downturn with the diagnosis of Neutropenia, a condition characterized by an abnormally low count of white blood cells, specifically neutrophils, crucial for fighting infections. This condition put him at risk of developing neutropenic sepsis, a life-threatening complication.

Despite his resilience, he experienced difficulty breathing, fatigue, and weakness, leading to another hospitalization.

With this new infection further complicating Elijah's already challenging journey, it became even more crucial for me to be by his side, advocating for his well-being, and providing the care and support he deserved.

As we journeyed through these challenging times together, I found solace in the realization that I could be there for Elijah, providing him with comfort, companionship, and unwavering support. Our bond had only grown stronger amidst adversity, and I had remained steadfast in my commitment to being his pillar of strength, regardless of what lay ahead.

Elijah's hospital stay this time lasted for a month. He appeared to be improving, but one day as I entered his room, I was alarmed to find him sweating profusely and barely able to speak about what was wrong. Rushing to the nurse's station for answers, I was directed to speak with the nurse in charge. Frustration and concern welled up inside me, and I addressed the nurse in a cold, demanding tone, insisting on immediate information about my husband's condition and questioning why I hadn't been contacted earlier.

Recognizing the urgency of the situation, the nurse quickly made a call. Meanwhile, I had already dialed Dr.

Goblieb, the doctor I trusted with Elijah's care. Fortunately, he was just arriving at the hospital and promptly made his way to Elijah's room. Our primary doctor was also present.

Gathering together, they invited me into the family waiting room. There, they disclosed that Elijah had developed an infection, and samples had been sent to the CDC in Atlanta for analysis. The uncertainty of the situation weighed heavily as they explained that Elijah was extremely ill, with his chances of survival slim. They asked if I comprehended the gravity of the situation.

"Yes, I understand what you're saying, and please don't think I'm in denial, but my husband is coming home with me. The God I serve, who is a healer, is telling me that."

They both just stared at me, their skepticism palpable. But in that moment, I knew deep in my heart that God had a plan—a plan that included Elijah's recovery.

I stayed with Elijah most of the night, my prayers mingling with the beeping of machines and the soft hum of the hospital ward. It was a long, agonizing vigil, but I refused to give in to despair. Home beckoned to me, a sanctuary of love and happiness where Elijah belonged.

And so, with a heavy heart but steadfast resolve, I made my way home. As I entered our bedroom, the familiar surroundings enveloped me in a warm embrace. I sank to my knees, the words of the 23rd Psalm spilling from my lips like a lifeline.

"The Lord is my shepherd; I shall not want. He maketh me to lie down in green pastures: he leadeth me beside the still waters. He restoreth my soul: he leadeth me in the paths of righteousness for his name's sake. Yea, though I walk through the valley of the shadow of death, I will fear no evil: for thou art with me; thy rod and thy staff they comfort me. Thou preparest a table before me in the presence of mine enemies: thou anointest my head with oil; my cup runneth over. Surely goodness and mercy shall follow me all the days of my life: and I will dwell in the house of the Lord forever."

And then I prayed like I've never prayed before, my words a desperate plea to the Heavenly Father.

"My Lord and savior Jesus Christ, I have been told that my husband Elijah is very ill and his chance for survival is very slim. Only you know if this is true because it is you and only you who hold the power of life and death in your hands. I pray that you'll remove this infection from his body.

In the Bible, I've read of your miraculous healing, and I believe you still heal the same way today. I also know from my experience of life on earth that not everyone is healed, and I also know that death is healing from all sickness. Lord, if it's your plan to take my husband, so be it if that is your will. Help me to understand your plan and help me to prepare myself for my husband's return to you if that is your will.

Father, I thank you that Elijah, who is extremely ill, belongs to you, and you are in control of everything that happens from our first breath to our last. But, Lord, I ask of you to please let me have him for just a little while longer. It is just him and me now. We raised our children; they are doing well. Elijah and I were enjoying ourselves, traveling and just being together."

In that moment of raw vulnerability, I surrendered myself to God's will, trusting that whatever the outcome, He would be with us every step of the way.

CHAPTER 5
A BEACON OF HOPE

As I opened my eyes, there was a bright light in my room, so blinding that I could barely see. Initially, I thought it was just the headlights from a passing bus illuminating the room, as the city bus often traversed down our street. But as I fully awakened, the realization struck me—I was on the second floor of my home, far too high for bus lights to reach. In that moment, I felt a divine presence, a reassurance from God that my beloved Elijah was going to be alright and coming home. "Thank you, Lord," I whispered as I settled into my bed.

The following morning, I arrived at the hospital early. Walking into Elijah's room, I was greeted by the sight of him looking remarkably better, able to converse with me. Elijah remained in the hospital for another three weeks.

On the day of Elijah's discharge, Dr. Goblieb coincidentally walked into the hospital just as I was bringing Elijah to the car. He remarked to Elijah, "Mr. Brown, you are a miracle." But I interjected, insisting that Elijah's recovery was not a miracle, but a testament to the miracle worker I believed in.

Quoting Isaiah 41:10, I reminded them both: "I will strengthen you and help you; I will uphold you with My righteous right hand." This scripture served as a poignant reminder that God is ever-present, offering strength and support through life's trials.

Dr. Goblieb, taken aback, simply nodded, and mentioned that he wanted to schedule a follow-up appointment with Elijah in his office the following week.

I didn't disclose to my children what the doctors had conveyed to me regarding the slim chance of Elijah's survival. Deep down, I knew he was coming home. In a moment of prayer, God reassured me with a blinding light in my room, conveying that everything would be alright.

Why didn't I tell them? Why did I keep this heartbreaking news from them when they had every right to know?

It wasn't because I wanted to deceive them or keep them in the dark. It wasn't because I was trying to shield them from the harsh reality of life, though a part of me desperately wanted to protect their hearts from breaking. No, the reason was much deeper than that. It was because, in that moment, I felt that my role was to be a beacon of light for my family, to hold onto hope when it seemed like all hope was lost. I wanted to give them something to believe in, something to hold onto, and I knew that telling them the doctor's prognosis would have snuffed out that light.

Our children were already facing the greatest challenge of their lives—watching their father, their hero, fade away before their eyes. They were struggling to understand why this was happening, why their strong and loving father was being taken away from them. I could see the fear in their eyes, the uncertainty, the quiet questions they dared not ask. I knew that if I told them the full extent of the doctor's words, it would crush the fragile sense of hope they were clinging to.

I wanted them to have faith. I wanted them to believe in miracles, to believe that their father could defy the odds, that God could still make a way where there seemed to be no way. I wanted them to keep praying, keep hoping, and keep loving with all their might. I wanted them to hold onto the belief that no matter what the doctors said, their father's fate was ultimately in God's hands. If loving their father and believing in his recovery was "wrong" by the world's standards, then I didn't want them to be "right." I wanted them to keep loving, keep believing, and keep fighting alongside him.

Keeping the truth to myself was not easy. It was a burden I carried silently, a weight that pressed down on my shoulder's day and night. There were moments when I wanted to cry out, to tell them everything, to share the pain that was tearing me apart inside. But I knew that doing so would only add to their suffering, would only make this journey even harder for them. And so, I chose to bear the weight alone, to keep the full truth hidden in the depths of my heart.

I remember sitting by Elijah's bedside late at night when the hospital was quiet and still. I would look at his face, so peaceful in sleep, and feel the tears welling up in my eyes. I would pray silently, asking God for strength, asking Him to give me the courage to face whatever was to come. I prayed not just for Elijah's healing, but for the strength to be the anchor my family needed me to be. I knew that my children were looking to me, taking their cues from my strength, my faith, my hope. I could not let them see the fear that gripped my heart, the doubts that crept into my mind late at night. I had to be strong—for them, for Elijah, and for myself.

There were days when it felt like I was living two different lives. On the outside, I was the pillar of strength, holding my family together, encouraging them to keep faith and keep fighting. But on the inside, I was a mother and a wife breaking under the weight of knowing that my husband's time with us was slipping away. I was caught between hope and despair, faith, and fear, wanting to believe in a miracle while also preparing for the worst.

As I look back now, I know that my decision to keep the truth from my children was not about denying reality. It was about choosing to hold onto light in the midst of darkness, to keep the flame of hope burning even when it seemed like the wind would blow it out. It was about protecting them, yes, but also about giving them the strength to keep going, to keep believing in the goodness of God, even when life seemed unbearably cruel.

Elijah's battle with cancer taught me many things, but perhaps the most important lesson was that: in the face of unimaginable pain and suffering, we must choose to be a beacon of light for those we love. We must choose to hold onto hope, even when the world tells us it is foolish. We must choose to believe in miracles, even when the odds are stacked against us. And we must choose to love fiercely and fully no matter how much it hurts, no matter how uncertain the future may be.

Looking back, I do not regret my decision. I know I did what I thought was best for our family, what I believed Elijah would have wanted. I chose to keep the light of hope alive, and I believe that in doing so, I honored his memory and the love we shared. And in the end, that is all I could do—love, hope, and believe, even in the darkest of times.

When Elijah finally returned home and his condition improved, I decided to share my faith-driven certainty with my children. Their reaction was unexpected; they were upset, questioning why I had not confided in them during those trying times. I simply explained that I did not want them to worry unnecessarily when I had absolute faith in God's promise. Elijah and I live in New York, while our daughter Carol resides just 15 minutes away. Despite this proximity, I refrained from burdening her emotionally, understanding that she had her own life to manage. Allen's family is in Pennsylvania, and Todd's family is in Virginia. Asking them to travel such distances for what I believed would be a positive outcome seemed unnecessary. My trust in God's plan guided my decisions throughout Elijah's ordeal.

CHAPTER 6
EMBRACING LIFE'S GIFTS

And so, in 2005, a new chapter in Elijah's journey began.

As the dawn of this New Year approached, a sense of renewal filled the air. Elijah's recovery had ushered in a new chapter in our lives, one filled with hope, gratitude, and a renewed zest for life.

As the months passed, it seemed as though a veil had been lifted, and the darkness of illness was replaced with the vibrant hues of joy and vitality. Our days were once again filled with laughter, adventure, and the simple pleasures of life.

As I sit down to share this chapter of our journey, I am filled with overwhelming gratitude and joy. It is hard to believe that three years have passed since Elijah's diagnosis, and now, I'm overjoyed to say that he is in remission. These years have been marked by so many ups and downs, but through every challenge, we clung to hope, and that hope carried us through. Now, we can finally embrace life again, and we have decided that it's time to fulfill the dreams we once put on hold, traveling to the places we've always longed to see.

One of the most incredible parts of this newfound freedom has been the ability to travel and explore the world together. Before Elijah's illness, we had dreams of seeing exotic destinations, and now, we're turning those dreams into reality.

Our first adventure took us to the beautiful islands of The Bahamas. The moment we stepped off the plane and felt the warm breeze on our faces, we knew that this trip would be the first of many unforgettable experiences. From swimming with dolphins to exploring hidden coves, every moment was a celebration of life and love.

Next, we jetted off to Hawaii, where we were greeted by towering mountains, lush jungles, and some of the most breathtaking beaches we had ever seen. We hiked to majestic waterfalls, danced at traditional luaus, and soaked in the aloha spirit that surrounded us at every turn.

Puerto Rico captured our hearts with its vibrant culture, colorful streets, and delicious cuisine. We wandered through historic Old San Juan, sipping on freshly squeezed mango juice as we listened to the rhythms of salsa music drifting through the air. And of course, no trip to Puerto Rico would be complete without a visit to the bioluminescent bay, where we kayaked under the stars, marveling at the glowing waters beneath us.

Bermuda charmed us with its pink sand beaches and pastel-colored houses dotting the coastline. We spent lazy days lounging on the sand, snorkeling in crystal-clear waters, and indulging in afternoon tea at quaint seaside cafes. Each day felt like a dream as we explored this enchanting island paradise.

But our adventures did not stop there. We were fortunate enough to embark on two cruises with friends and family, sailing to the tropical paradises of Barbados and the United Virgin Islands. Cruising through the azure waters, we laughed, danced, and created memories that would last a lifetime.

In Barbados, we explored lush rainforests, swam with sea turtles, and sampled the island's famous rum punch. And in the United Virgin Islands, we snorkeled among vibrant coral reefs, hiked to hidden waterfalls, and danced the night away under the stars.

Our final destination was Aruba, where we were greeted by endless sunshine, gentle trade winds, and some of the friendliest people we had ever met. We swam in turquoise waters, went horseback riding along the coast, and marveled at the stunning sunsets that painted the sky in shades of orange and pink.

As I reflect on these past beautiful years, I am reminded of the power of resilience, love, and the human spirit. Despite the challenges we faced, we never lost sight of our dreams, and now, we're living them to the fullest.

This chapter of our journey is a testament to the beauty of life's unexpected twists and turns, and the joy that awaits us when we embrace each moment with open hearts and grateful souls.

We embarked on countless journeys, each one a testament to the resilience of the human spirit and the power of love to conquer even the greatest of challenges. From the sun-kissed shores of Puerto Rico to the tropical paradise of Hawaii, we reveled in the beauty of the world around us, savoring each moment as if it were a precious gift.

But it wasn't just the exotic destinations that brought us joy—it was the simple act of being together, hand in hand, exploring new horizons and creating memories that would last a lifetime. Whether we were lounging on the beaches of the US Virgin Islands or marveling at the majestic beauty of America's national parks, each adventure was a celebration of life and love.

As the years passed, our travels took us everywhere, from the bustling streets of New York City to the serene landscapes of the Pacific Northwest. But no matter where we went, one thing remained constant: our love for each other and our unwavering gratitude for the gift of life.

Now in 2009, as we reflected on the journey that had brought us to this moment, we realized just how far we had come. Against all odds, we had emerged stronger, more resilient, and more deeply connected than ever before. Elijah had now been in remission for four years.

And so, as we looked ahead to the future, we did so with hearts full of hope and gratitude, knowing that no matter what challenges lay ahead, we would face them together, hand in hand, with a love that knew no bounds.

CHAPTER 7
BLESSED YEARS TOGETHER: CHERISHING FAMILY, FAITH, AND SPORTS

Life had settled into a beautiful rhythm once again. We were both retired; Elijah and I found ourselves with ample time to cherish each other's company, surrounded by the laughter and love of our children, grandchildren, and great-grandchildren. It was a testament to God's abundant blessings upon our lives.

Our son Allen and his wife Melissa had welcomed their first child, a beautiful baby boy. And in a touching tribute to Elijah, they had chosen to honor him by naming their son after him. The legacy of Elijah would live on through the next generation, a testament to his enduring impact on our family. They would have three more sons. Isaiah, Josiah, and Micaiah.

Meanwhile, our son Todd and his wife Kimmy had their own bundles of joy. Quiana, Keyron, Brianna, their fourth daughter, was named Camille Carolyn. And their fifth daughter Kayla .Our Great Grand Children. Caliyah, King, Dominque, Kallie, Kahlil, Kaysen, and Kamora.

With the arrival of grandchildren, Elijah took on the endearing title of "PaPa," while I was lovingly called "Grammy." Our family flourished, and Elijah's warmth and affection endeared him to all.

With each new addition to our family, our hearts expanded with love and wonder, marveling at the miracle of life and the blessings that surrounded us.

In those moments, surrounded by the love of our growing family, I could not help but feel overwhelmed with happiness. Our journey together had been marked by moments of triumph and challenges, but through it all, our family remained a source of strength and light.

And as we continued our journey, I carried with me a heart full of gratitude and love, knowing that no matter what the future held, our family would always be our greatest blessing.

Elijah's passion for sports knew no bounds. From baseball to hockey, tennis to soccer, he embraced every game with unbridled enthusiasm. Whether cheering with our grandsons at Mets or Yankees games or supporting our granddaughters in their endeavors, Elijah's excitement was contagious. It seemed as though the kids adored him; I thought even more than they did me at times!

Our nieces and nephews also felt Elijah's unwavering support. Whenever they had games or events, Elijah was the first to say, "Let's go!" His dedication knew no bounds, even extending to his lone nephew Troy, whom he made sure felt included in our family outings.

These years were truly a blessing. In addition to our family life, Elijah and I served as pillars of our church community. With multiple responsibilities, including Elijah's roles as church controller, singer in the male and senior choirs. As Deacons, we found ourselves busy but fulfilled. Elijah's leadership was evident in every aspect, and his ability to solve problems with grace and wisdom earned him the respect of all who knew him.

Together, we navigated the joys and challenges of life, grateful for each moment spent in the embrace of family, faith, and the shared love of sports.

In the tranquil state of our marriage, all seemed to be well. Elijah diligently attended his medical appointments, and I took solace in believing that everything was under control. As we celebrated our 36th Wedding Anniversary, our hearts overflowed with gratitude and joy. We could not have been happier, basking in the warmth of our enduring love and the blessings of our shared journey. I prayed:

Heavenly Father,

I come before you today with a heart brimming with gratitude and thanksgiving. I lift up my voice in praise for the abundant blessings you have bestowed upon us, especially for the gift of Elijah's well-being and presence in our lives.

Lord, I am profoundly thankful for the precious moments we share as a family, for the laughter that fills our home, and for the love that binds us together. In your infinite mercy and grace, you have watched over Elijah, guiding him through each day with strength and resilience.

Thank you, Lord, for the skilled hands of the doctors and the wisdom of the medical professionals who have cared for him. I am grateful for their expertise and dedication, which have played a vital role in his journey to health and wholeness.

As we gather together, surrounded by the love of family and friends, I am reminded of your faithfulness and goodness. Your presence sustains us through every trial and triumph, and for that, we are eternally grateful.

Lord, continue to bless Elijah with health, vitality, and strength. May your loving arms surround him, shielding him from harm and filling his heart with peace. Grant him the courage to face each day with faith and hope, knowing that you are by his side.

Thank you, Lord, for the precious gift of Elijah's life and for the countless blessings you continue to pour out upon us. May our hearts overflow with gratitude and praise as we cherish each moment together as a family. In your holy name, Amen.

At this point in our lives, everything seemed to have settled back into a comforting sense of normalcy. Elijah's health was thriving, and each day brought with it a renewed sense of gratitude for the blessings we had received. Little did I know that a simple request from Elijah would soon lead us on an unexpected journey filled with memories and revelations?

It was a typical day when Elijah approached me with a surprising proposition. He spoke with a gleam in his eyes, a spark of nostalgia igniting within him. "Would you be interested in taking a small vacation?" he asked, his voice filled with excitement. "I'd like to visit my birthplace in Charleston, South Carolina."

I could not help but feel taken aback by his request. After all, Elijah's family had left Charleston when he was just seven years old, and I had not anticipated a trip back to his roots. Nevertheless, I could see the longing in his eyes, the desire to reconnect with his past. And so, without hesitation, I replied, "Okay, when do you want to go? I'll call the airline to make reservations."

But Elijah had a different idea in mind. "No," he said, a smile playing at the corners of his lips. "Let's drive."

The thought of embarking on a road trip from New York to South Carolina seemed daunting, to say the least.

A journey of ten to twelve hours by car was no small feat, especially considering our age. But Elijah's enthusiasm was infectious, and I found myself agreeing to his proposal without a second thought.

"We can leave New York and visit your mother in Virginia," he suggested, his eyes alight with anticipation. "We'll spend a few days with her, and then we can make our way to North Carolina to visit our friends who recently moved there. From there, it's just a short drive to South Carolina, where we can visit our nephew Norman and your cousin Martha."

His plan sounded like the adventure of a lifetime, a chance to explore new places and revisit cherished memories along the way. And so, with a sense of excitement and anticipation, we began to make preparations for our upcoming journey.

Little did I know that this road trip would not only lead us to Elijah's birthplace but also to unexpected discoveries and heartfelt connections that would leave a lasting impact on our lives.

About two weeks after that memorable conversation, Elijah and I embarked on our journey to explore his birthplace. Following his plan, we first made our way to Virginia to surprise my mother. Keeping our visit a secret was my idea, and the joy on her face when she opened the door to find us standing there was worth every bit of the effort. Little did I know that this would be one of the last times I would surprise her, as she passed away the following year. But in that moment, her smile was all that mattered.

From Virginia, we traveled to North Carolina to visit our friends, who were equally delighted to see us. After spending two wonderful days catching up with them, we continued on our journey to South Carolina, our final destination.

As always, I took on the role of the driver, and I found great enjoyment in navigating the roads as we journeyed southward. Arriving at our hotel in the early evening, we took a leisurely stroll around the area before retiring for the night, eager for the adventures that awaited us in the morning.

The next day, Elijah was filled with excitement, eager to explore the familiar streets of his childhood. Over breakfast at a cozy little restaurant, he amused me with stories of his memories from when he was just seven years old.

As we ventured out into the city, it amazed me how he could recall details from so long ago, pointing out landmarks and buildings that held special significance to him.

Elijah led the way, guiding me to places that he remembered from his youth. Though much had changed over the years, he was able to show me where his family had once lived, his grandmother's house still standing as a testament to the passage of time.

For three days, we immersed ourselves in the sights and sounds of South Carolina, driving from the bustling city to the tranquil countryside. We visited my cousin and our nephew, sharing the joy of reconnecting with loved ones and exploring the beauty of the land.

Before we left on Sunday, we attended a worship service at the church his family had belonged to. As I sat beside Elijah, I could not help but marvel at the depth of his memories and the significance of our journey together. Though I could not fathom how he remembered so much after all these years, I was grateful for the opportunity to be by his side, witnessing the joy and wonder in his eyes.

As we journeyed back towards New York, our adventure took an unexpected turn. Just as we were approaching our home state, my cell phone rang, interrupting the peaceful hum of the road. It was my niece on the line, her voice heavy with worry as she informed me that her daughter had fallen ill and had been admitted to the hospital. Without hesitation, Elijah and I made the decision to change our plans and head towards Washington D.C. to be with them.

Our detour to the nation's capital was brief but filled with moments of heartfelt connection and love. Despite the circumstances that brought us there, it was a pleasure to reunite with my nieces and offer our support in their time of need. As we embraced each other I felt a sense of unity and strength in our family bond.

Together, we spent a few precious hours together, sharing stories, laughter, and prayers. In the quiet moments of reflection, we found solace in each other's presence, drawing strength from our shared faith and love for one another. It was a reminder of the importance of family, of being there for each other through the highs and lows of life's journey.

Our stay in Washington D.C. may have been brief, but it left a permanent mark on my heart. It was a reminder of the power of love and the importance of cherishing every moment we have with those we hold dear. And as we resumed our journey back to New York, I carried with me a renewed sense of appreciation for the blessings of family and the strength that comes from being united in love.

This adventure was a testament to the enduring bond between us, a journey filled with love, laughter, and cherished memories. And as we made our way back home, I knew in my heart that this trip would forever hold a special place in my heart, a testament to the enduring love that had carried us through the years.

CHAPTER 8
A RETURN TO NORMALCY, A RETURN OF FEAR

As we settled back into the familiar rhythms of home, it felt as though we had returned from a whirlwind of adventures that had taken us across the world. From exploring Elijah's birthplace to visiting friends and family, our journey had been filled with moments of joy, gratitude, and cherished memories. Yet, amidst the backdrop of our seemingly idyllic life, there lingered a silent fear, a fear that had once been vanquished but now threatened to resurface.

In the quiet moments of reflection, I found myself thanking God for the blessings we had received. Despite the challenges we had faced, we had emerged stronger and more resilient than ever before.

Elijah's health had seemed to be on an upward trajectory, and I had allowed myself to believe that the worst was behind us. But as we settled back into our routine, signs began to emerge that all was not as it seemed.

Elijah's once vibrant energy began to wane, replaced by a sense of fatigue and slowness. He would sleep late into the morning, struggling to find the strength to face the day ahead. And as he attempted to move about the house, I noticed a subtle stiffness in his walk, a hesitation that spoke volumes.

I knew in my heart what these signs meant, even before the words were spoken aloud. The cancer had returned, its insidious presence lurking just beneath the surface, threatening to disrupt our lives once again. With a heavy heart, I mentioned the subject to Elijah, urging him to see the doctor and seek the medical attention he needed.

Since Elijah was in remission, he has been seeing Dr. Goblieb every six weeks, unless new issues arise. Dr. Goblieb recently informed us that he may soon be leaving to take on the role of Chief of Staff at a nearby hospital. When that happens, he has assured us that he would recommend a highly qualified doctor to continue overseeing Elijah's care.

When we contacted Dr. Goblieb's office, we were informed that he had moved on as mentioned to a new position as Chief of Staff at another hospital, and his patients had been transferred to a different doctor. The news sent a shiver down my spine as I grappled with the uncertainty of who would now be responsible for Elijah's care.

In that moment, the illusion of normalcy shattered, replaced by a sense of fear and apprehension. Our lives had once again been thrust into uncertainty, and I found myself grappling with questions that had no easy answers. But amidst the turmoil, one thing remained constant – our faith in God's guiding hand, and the belief that He would see us through whatever trials lay ahead.

As we prepared to face this new chapter in our journey, I clung to the hope that had sustained us through the darkest of days. And though the road ahead may be troubled with challenges, I knew that with faith, love, and unwavering determination, we would overcome whatever obstacles stood in our way.

With Dr. Goblieb no longer overseeing Elijah's treatment, a wave of uncertainty swept over us. However, Dr. Goblieb had not left us adrift; instead, he had ensured a smooth transition by referring us to another oncologist whom he trusted implicitly. This new beacon of hope in our medical journey was Dr. Finkleman. With a sense of relief and gratitude, we promptly scheduled an appointment to meet with him the following week.

The assurance of Dr. Goblieb's recommendation brought a glimmer of hope amidst the uncertainty that had clouded our minds. We trusted in his judgment and expertise, knowing that he would not lead us astray in such a critical matter. As we awaited our meeting with Dr. Finkleman, a sense of cautious optimism began to take root within us, mingled with a determination to face whatever lay ahead with courage and resilience.

In the days leading up to our appointment, we found solace in the knowledge that we were in capable hands. Though the road ahead remained uncertain, we took comfort in the fact that we were not alone in our journey. With faith, hope, and the support of our loved ones, we prepared ourselves to confront the challenges that lay ahead, knowing that we would emerge stronger on the other side.

As we anticipated our initial meeting with this doctor, we're earnestly praying for his guidance in shedding light on Elijah's condition: So, I prayed.

Lord, we humbly ask for Your divine wisdom and discernment to rest upon this doctor who will be providing insight into Elijah's health. Guide his hands and thoughts as he delves into the complexities of Elijah's illness. Grant him clarity and understanding as he reviews test results and formulates the optimal treatment strategy.

We pray that You surround him with Your peace and grace, allowing him to be a vessel of Your healing power. May his decisions be guided by compassion and knowledge, leading to the best possible outcome for Elijah. We trust in Your infinite wisdom and loving care, knowing that with You, all things are possible.

In Jesus' name, we pray. Amen.

Our meeting with Dr. Finkleman was marked by a sense of anticipation and apprehension as we awaited his expert assessment of Elijah's condition. From the moment we stepped into his office, we were greeted with warmth and professionalism, instantly putting us at ease.

Dr. Finkleman wasted no time in conducting a thorough examination of Elijah, mirroring the meticulous approach we had come to expect from Dr. Goblieb. With precision and care, he reviewed Elijah's medical history and carefully examined him, leaving no stone unturned in his quest for answers.

As we sat in the examination room, Elijah and I exchanged nervous glances, silently praying for positive news. Yet, amidst the uncertainty that hung in the air, there was a sense of reassurance in Dr. Finkleman's confident demeanor. His expertise and experience were evident as he meticulously reviewed Elijah's medical records, familiarizing himself with the intricacies of his case.

With a reassuring smile, Dr. Finkleman assured us that he would leave no stone unturned in his quest for answers. He explained that he would need to await the results of various tests and scans before formulating a comprehensive treatment plan. However, he emphasized that he would expedite the process, recognizing the urgency of Elijah's situation.

As we left Dr. Finkleman's office, we felt a mix of hope and apprehension. We awaited his call and took comfort in knowing Elijah was in capable hands.

Dr. Finkleman's dedication to Elijah's care gave us confidence, and we were reassured that, no matter what the future held, we would face it together with strength, resilience, and unwavering faith.

Within a few days, the anticipated call came, summoning us back to Dr. Finkleman's office. As we sat before him, the weight of worry and concern hung heavy in the air, casting a somber shadow over the room. We knew, deep down, what the results would reveal even before a single word left his lips.

With a heavy heart, Dr. Finkleman delivered the news we had dreaded hearing – the cancer had returned. His words echoed in the silence that followed, the weight of their implication settling upon us like a suffocating blanket. Despite our hopes and prayers, the reality of Elijah's condition loomed large before us, casting a cloud over our once bright future.

In that moment, time seemed to stand still as we coped with the harsh reality of our circumstances. The familiar sting of fear and uncertainty gnawed at our hearts, threatening to overwhelm us with despair. Yet, amidst the darkness that threatened to engulf us, a flicker of determination ignited within us, a determination to face this new battle head-on with courage and resolve.

As we left Dr. Finkleman's office, the weight of his words hung heavily upon our shoulders, but we refused to be consumed by despair. Though the road ahead would be tense with challenges and obstacles, we vowed to navigate it together, drawing strength from the love and support that surrounded us.

CHAPTER 9
STRENGTH IN SICKNESS:
A JOURNEY OF LOVE AND RESILIENCE

Once again, Elijah found himself faced with a difficult decision, one that would shape the course of his treatment and, ultimately, his journey towards healing. With the cancer returning, he was presented with the option of radiation or infusion therapy. After careful consideration and consultation with his medical team, Elijah chose infusion therapy, determined to face this new battle with courage and resilience.

And so, the treatments began, each session taking its toll on Elijah's already weakened body. As he grew increasingly frail, I stepped into the role of his devoted caregiver, accompanying him not only to his treatments but to any place he needed or wanted to go.

Despite his own struggles, Elijah remained determined to maintain a sense of normalcy in his life. He insisted on going grocery shopping every Thursday night after choir rehearsal, relishing the quiet solitude of the nearly empty store. I would go with him.

With each passing day, Elijah's strength waned, the effects of the cancer and the intensive treatments taking their toll on his body. Yet, amidst the physical pain and discomfort, he remained the epitome of strength and resilience, a testament to the strong spirit that defined him.

Despite his own suffering, Elijah's thoughts were always for me, his concern for my well-being concealing any consideration for his own. He would often apologize for the burden he believed he was placing on me; expressing gratitude for all that I did to care for him.

In those moments of vulnerability, I found solace in the vows we had exchanged on our wedding day, promising to stand by each other through thick and thin, in sickness and in health. As I repeated those solemn words to him, I was reminded of the depth of our love and the strength of our commitment to one another.

Through it all, Elijah remained the rock upon which I leaned, his unwavering love and support sustaining me through the darkest of days. And though our journey was troubled with challenges and obstacles, I knew that as long as we faced them together, we could weather any storm that came our way.

Facing Elijah's cancer diagnosis had been one of the most daunting experiences in our lives, but it is often in these moments of profound challenge that we discover our deepest reservoirs of strength. Each day brings new hurdles, from the physical toll of treatments to the emotional and mental strain, yet within these trials lays the opportunity for growth and resilience.

Embracing each day with courage, Elijah finds solace in the unwavering support of our loved ones, the expertise of his medical team, and the small victories that signify progress, no matter how. gradual

Drawing on his faith, inner strength, and the power of a positive mindset, Elijah had found a renewed sense of purpose and determination. We learn to appreciate the present moment, finding joy in simple pleasures and comfort in the steady rhythms of life. This journey, though difficult, had revealed a determined spirit in Elijah that not only aided in his battle against illness but also inspired all of us around him. Through the lens of strength and hope, Elijah's fight against cancer becomes not just a struggle, but a testament to human endurance and the enduring power of hope.

CHAPTER 10
FORTY-ONE YEARS OF LOVE AND COURAGE

It was the year 2002 when our lives were forever changed. Elijah, my beloved husband, was diagnosed with cancer. The news hit us like a freight train, and we were thrown into a world we never imagined entering. The initial shock slowly turned into a relentless fight, as we faced this new, terrifying chapter together.

By 2005, the prognosis became grim. Doctors informed us that Elijah's chances of survival were slim. The cancer was aggressive, and it seemed like the odds were stacked against him. Elijah was admitted to the Intensive Care Unit, where he spent two harrowing weeks battling for his life. It was a time filled with uncertainty and fear, each day blurring into the next. After ICU, he was transferred to a regular hospital room, where he remained for another month. We clung to every small sign of progress, every tiny victory that suggested he might pull through.

Against all odds, Elijah overcame this critical phase. He emerged from the hospital, not just alive, but with a renewed spirit that surprised even the doctors. His remarkable recovery continued, and eventually, he went into remission. Though we knew the odds were against us, God granted us nine more precious years together—years we cherished as a gift.

For nine precious years, we enjoyed life with a sense of normalcy we had almost forgotten. We traveled, laughed, and cherished every moment as if it were a gift. But happiness would not last forever. In 2014, the reality we had been dreading began to unfold. The cancer resurfaced, bringing with it a new wave of challenges.

Elijah began infusion therapy; a grueling process repeated every three weeks. Each session required him to sit in the clinic for an hour while the medication was administered. The treatment took a heavy toll on his body. Fever and chills became frequent companions. He lost weight rapidly, his once-strong frame withering away. Nausea, vomiting, and diarrhea plagued him, adding to his misery. Pain in his muscles and joints became a constant, gnawing ache that no medication seemed able to ease.

One particularly difficult day, after a routine oncologist appointment, Elijah returned home unable to walk. The pain was so severe that he had to be hospitalized again. For three weeks, he remained in the hospital, receiving intensive care to manage his symptoms and regain some strength. Slowly, he began to improve, enough that his medical team felt he could benefit from rehabilitation. On April 10, 2014, Elijah was transferred to a rehabilitation facility. I believed this was a positive step, a sign that he was on the path to recovery.

To me, rehab meant restoration, a return to a semblance of normalcy. Elijah needed therapy to help him walk again, to regain his strength and independence. I visited the facility every day, watching closely as he participated in physical therapy and other activities. He seemed to be recovering well, and my heart swelled with hope. I envisioned the day he would come home, where we could continue our life together, where he could heal in the comfort of our own space.

But that day never came. On April 28, 2014, my world was shattered. My husband of forty-one years, my partner, my friend, lost his battle with cancer.

The man who had fought so bravely, who had faced every challenge with courage and strength, was gone. I was left with a deep void, a heart heavy with grief, and memories of our time together. Elijah had been my rock, my anchor. His loss was more than I could bear.

In those final days, I learned the true meaning of resilience, love, and loss. Elijah's journey through cancer was one of courage, a testament to his strength and determination. Though he is no longer with me, his spirit remains a guiding light, a reminder of the love we shared and the battles we fought together. His memory lives on in my heart, and in every moment, we were blessed to have.

CHAPTER 11
WE NEVER SAY GOODBYE:
WE SAY SEE YOU LATER

April 28, 2014—a date that will forever be etched in my heart. It was the day I lost Elijah, my beloved husband, the day our battle with cancer came to a devastating end. I remember that day with a clarity that feels like a wound that never fully heals. It began like any other, with a mixture of hope and anxiety as I made my way to the rehab facility where Elijah had been staying. But as soon as I arrived, I knew something was terribly wrong.

As I approached Elijah's room, my eyes were immediately drawn to the two large oxygen tanks stationed beside his bed. He was wearing an oxygen mask, his breathing shallow and labored. My heart dropped. Fighting the wave of dread that washed over me, I called out softly, "Elijah, I'm here," but there was no response. Panic surged through me as the gravity of the situation became clear. Why hadn't anyone called me? Why hadn't I been told about this sudden turn? Overwhelmed, I rushed out of the room, frantically searching for a nurse.

When I found the nurse, I demanded an explanation. "What happened? Why wasn't I or any family member informed about his condition?" My voice trembled with urgency. I insisted that Elijah needed to be transferred to a hospital immediately and told her to call for an emergency vehicle. She looked at me with a mix of concern and helplessness, explaining that a doctor's approval was required for discharge. But I was not willing to wait.

I took charge of the situation, pulling out my phone and making the call myself. As his wife, I knew I had the authority to make decisions about his care, and in that critical moment, I knew Elijah needed the advanced care only a hospital could provide. Time was of the essence, and I was not going to let bureaucracy stand in the way of his well-being.

Every second felt like an eternity. I kept thinking about Elijah lying there, struggling for breath, and I knew I needed to get him the help he deserved, the help he needed.

I had called my niece Michele, who is a nurse practitioner, she came before the emergency vehicle got there and she immediately began asking the critical questions, her voice calm but commanding. She demanded to know why Elijah hadn't been transferred to a hospital as soon as his condition started to deteriorate, stating he should have been already. There were so many medical questions she asked, there were no answers as to why he wasn't rushed to the hospital or why the family wasn't called.

My sister Doris arrived shortly after, her presence a comforting support amid the chaos.

Every second felt like an eternity. I kept thinking about Elijah lying there, struggling for breath, and I knew I needed to get him the help he deserved, the help he needed.

When the EMS team finally arrived, it felt like a lifetime had passed. As they prepared to move Elijah, I stayed by his side, holding his hand and speaking softly to him. "Elijah, I'm here. I've got you." It was something we often said to each other, a promise of unwavering support and love. In our marriage, whenever one of us was hurting or unwell, the other would always say, "I've got you." It was our way of saying, "You're not alone; I'm here with you."

The ride to the hospital felt endless. The ambulance driver got lost, and every twist and turn seemed to drag out the journey. I kept talking to Elijah, trying to reassure him, even though I didn't know if he could hear me. I kept saying, "Hold on, Elijah. I'm right here. I've got you." I prayed silently, begging God to give us more time, just a little more time to be together.

When we finally reached the hospital, my sister and niece were already there, waiting anxiously. I immediately called our children—our daughter Carol and our sons, Todd, and Allen—and Elijah's sisters, to let them know what was happening. The doctor in charge came over and explained the situation, mentioning that Elijah had a DNR (Do Not Resuscitate) order in his records. He looked at me and asked, "What would you like to do?"

I had promised Elijah I would honor his wishes. He had been clear with me—he didn't want to be hooked up to machines, didn't want to be kept alive if there was no hope of recovery. As much as it tore me apart, I knew I had to respect his decision. I looked at the doctor and nodded. "Follow his wishes," I whispered, my voice barely holding steady.

By then, Carol had arrived in the emergency room. She took over, speaking with the doctors and calling her brothers to keep them updated. Todd and his wife, Kimmy, were in Virginia. As soon as they heard the news, they dropped everything, not even packing a bag, and got in their car to drive straight to New York. Allen, his wife Melissa, and their sons, Elijah, Isaiah, Josiah, and Micaiah, were on their way from Pennsylvania.

Carol and I stood on either side of Elijah's bed, holding his hands and talking to him, letting him know he wasn't alone. I began to reminisce about our life together, telling him what a wonderful husband and father he had been. I talked about the first time we met; about all the beautiful moments we had shared. I didn't know if he could hear me, but I needed him to know he wasn't alone. Tears streamed down my face as I pleaded with him, "Elijah, please, let me know you know I'm here. Honey, open your eyes. Please, just open your eyes and let me know you know I am here. Carol is here. Allen and Todd are on their way. Please, I begged, open your eyes, I am here, Michele and Doris are here. You are not alone."

For a moment, it felt like time stood still. Then, slowly, Elijah opened his eyes. My heart both broke and soared at the same time. He knew I was there. I laid my head gently on his chest, holding him close, whispering words of love and comfort, talking about our journey, our love, and our faith.

The nurse administered medication to try to keep his heart beating until more family could arrive. She asked how far away the nearest relatives were, and Carol quickly relayed the information. "Allen is at the Throgs Neck

Bridge—he's about 15 minutes away," she said. But Todd, coming from Virginia, was still far.

I kept my head on Elijah's chest, listening to his heartbeat, feeling each rise and fall of his breath. I glanced up at the monitor occasionally, watching as the numbers slowly declined. Each drop was a countdown, a ticking clock reminding me that our time was slipping away. I held onto him tighter, telling him repeatedly how much I loved him, how much he meant to me, how grateful I was for every moment we had shared.

Then, the numbers reached a critical low. I knew it was only a matter of seconds before the monitor would emit that steady, unforgiving beep—the sound of a life ending. Just as the long, flat tone filled the room, Allen and his family walked in, just five minutes too late. Elijah had taken his last breath.

My heart shattered in that moment, but I felt a strange sense of peace. Elijah wasn't suffering anymore. He wasn't in pain. He was free. And even though he was gone, I knew he had heard me, that he had felt our love surrounding him as he left this world. I had kept my promise to him, and now, all I could do was hold on to the memories, the love, and the unbreakable bond we shared.

That day, April 28, 2014, was the hardest day of my life. But it was also a day that reminded me of the depth of love, the strength of family, and the enduring power of faith. Elijah may have lost his battle with cancer, but he won the ultimate victory—peace in the arms of the Lord. We never say goodbye; we say see you later. And I know, one day, we will meet again.

CHAPTER 12
BY HIS SIDE: THE EARLY DAYS

The Cancer diagnosis had come like a bolt of lightning, shattering the calm of our lives. Cancer, a single word, but one that carried the weight of the world. My husband, Elijah, my rock, my confidant, my everything, was facing this terrifying battle. As his wife, I was thrust into the role of caregiver, supporter, and advocate. I had to find a way to cope with this illness that was part of our lives, and I needed to do it with grace, strength, and unwavering love.

In those early days after the diagnosis, I felt a wave of emotions that I could barely control. Fear, sadness, anger, and helplessness all coursed through me, sometimes all at once. But I knew I couldn't afford to let them consume me. Elijah needed me now more than ever, and I had to be strong for him. I decided that our journey with cancer would not be one of despair but of hope and resilience.

I started by educating myself about Elijah's specific type of cancer, understanding the treatment options, and learning about the side effects he might experience. I spoke with his doctors, asked countless questions, and read every piece of literature I could find. Knowledge, I realized, was power. It gave me a sense of control in a situation where so much was uncontrollable. More importantly, it allowed me to be a better advocate for Elijah, to understand what he was going through, and to make informed decisions about his care.

Every doctor's appointment, every test, every chemotherapy session became a battlefield, and I was determined to be by Elijah's side through it all. I knew he was the one fighting cancer, but I wanted him to know he wasn't fighting it alone. We were in this together, hand in hand, heart to heart.

I quickly learned that one of the most important things I could do was to stay positive. There were days when Elijah was too weak to get out of bed, days when the pain was so intense it brought him to tears, and days when the fear of the unknown was almost too much to bear. On those days, I made it my mission to be the light in his darkness. I would sit by his side, hold his hand, and remind him of all the reasons we had to keep fighting. I would tell him stories, share memories of our happiest moments, and talk about the future we were still planning to build together.

But it wasn't just about being strong and positive; it was also about being realistic. I knew I couldn't do it all on my own, and I had to take care of myself to take care of Elijah. I reached out to friends and family for support, accepting their offers to help with meals, errands, or just to be there for a chat. I joined a support group for spouses of cancer patients, where I found a community of people who understood exactly what I was going through. Talking to others who were facing similar challenges was incredibly comforting. It reminded me that I wasn't alone in this journey and that there was a network of people who could offer advice, support, and a listening ear.

Through it all, I discovered strength within myself that I never knew I had. I learned that coping with a loved one's illness doesn't mean being perfect; it means being present. It means showing up every day, even when you're tired, scared, or overwhelmed. It means finding moments of joy and laughter amidst the pain and sorrow. It means loving fiercely, holding onto hope, and believing in the possibility of a better tomorrow.

I also learned the importance of grace—grace for myself and grace for Elijah. There were days when I was short-tempered, days when I cried uncontrollably, and days when I felt like giving up. And there were days when Elijah felt the same. But through it all, we gave each other grace. We allowed ourselves to feel whatever we needed to feel and to express it without judgment. We knew that this was a marathon, not a sprint, and that we were allowed to have bad days. What mattered was that we kept moving forward, together.

Prayer became a cornerstone of my strength. Every night, I would kneel beside our bed and pray for Elijah's healing, for strength, for wisdom, and for peace. I prayed for the doctors and nurses who cared for him and for all the other families going through similar struggles. And I felt a sense of peace in those moments of prayer, a reminder that we were not alone in this battle and that there was a higher power guiding us through.

Elijah, too, drew strength from his faith. We would often pray together, holding hands and speaking words of hope and healing into the universe. Our faith became a source of comfort and a reminder that we were part of something greater than ourselves. It gave us the courage to face each day, no matter how difficult.

As the weeks turned into months, we began to find a new normal. Elijah's treatments were tough, but he was tougher. We found ways to incorporate small moments of joy into our days—watching a funny movie, sitting in our back yard where Elijah had planted beautiful flowers where we would have a meal, or he would read or simply holding each other close. We learned to celebrate the small victories, like a good day with minimal pain or a positive test result. Each moment of light was a reminder that there was still so much to be thankful for.

Through it all, my love for Elijah grew deeper than I ever thought possible. I realized that true love isn't just about the good times; it's about standing by each other's side through the darkest storms. It's about being a partner in every sense of the word, sharing in the struggles as well as the joys, and never giving up on each other.

Cancer may have brought us to our knees, but it also brought us closer together. It taught us the value of each moment, the strength of our love, and the power of hope. And as we continued this journey, I know that we were stronger for it. Together, we were facing the storm, hand in hand, with unwavering love and unyielding faith.

CHAPTER 13
THE SILENT DESTROYER: HOW CANCER TEARS FAMILIES APART

Cancer. Just the word alone can send a chill down your spine. It's a diagnosis no one wants to hear, a battle no one wants to fight. Yet, for so many, it becomes an unwelcome reality—a relentless force that invades lives, disrupts routines, and tears families apart. As I write this, I can't help but think about how profoundly cancer has affected my own life and the lives of those I love. It's a journey marked by pain, uncertainty, and grief, leaving scars that run deep.

Cancer is a silent destroyer. It creeps into your life when you least expect it, often without warning. A routine doctor's visit, a seemingly harmless symptom, and suddenly your world is turned upside down. The moment of diagnosis is like a punch to the gut—a feeling of disbelief mixed with fear and confusion. You hear the doctor's words, but they don't quite register. "Cancer." It's as if time stands still, and you are thrust into a nightmare from which you cannot wake.

From the moment of diagnosis, life becomes a whirlwind of medical appointments, tests, and treatments. Words like "chemotherapy," "radiation," and "biopsy" become part of your daily vocabulary. You learn to navigate the sterile corridors of hospitals and clinics, each visit filled with anxiety and dread. The treatments, though necessary, often feel like a battle within a battle—a fight not just against the disease but also against the side effects that ravage the body and spirit. You watch as your loved one endures pain, fatigue, and nausea, their strength slowly waning. The person you once knew begins to change before your eyes, and there's nothing you can do to stop it.

But cancer doesn't just attack the body; it attacks the very fabric of family life. It's not just the patient who suffers, but everyone around them. Family dynamics shift under the weight of the diagnosis. Roles change, responsibilities increase, and the emotional toll can be overwhelming. Suddenly, the everyday concerns of life—work, school, social activities—become secondary to the all-consuming focus on survival. Every decision, every plan is made with cancer in mind. It becomes the unwanted guest at every family gathering, the shadow over every conversation, the constant presence in every thought.

The emotional impact of cancer is profound. Fear becomes a constant companion. Fear of the unknown, fear of losing a loved one, fear of what the future holds. It's a fear that grips your heart and doesn't let go. There are days when the weight of it all feels unbearable—when the tears come without warning, and the despair feels too heavy to bear. You try to be strong, to put on a brave face for the sake of your loved one, but inside, you feel like you're falling apart.

Cancer also brings with it a sense of helplessness. You want to do something, anything, to make it go away, to ease the pain, to bring back a sense of normalcy. But there's nothing you can do except be there—to hold a hand, to offer a comforting word, to sit in silence and share in the suffering. You feel powerless in the face of a disease that shows no mercy. You pray for a miracle, for a breakthrough, for something to give you hope. But sometimes, all you can do is wait and hope for the best, knowing that the outcome is out of your control.

The financial burden of cancer is another harsh reality. Medical bills pile up, even with insurance, and the costs of treatments, medications, and hospital stays can be overwhelming. Many families find themselves in financial distress, forced to make difficult choices between paying for treatment and covering everyday expenses. The added stress of financial strain only compounds the emotional and physical toll of the disease, creating a perfect storm of suffering and despair.

Cancer doesn't just take a physical and financial toll; it takes a spiritual toll as well. It challenges your faith, your beliefs, your understanding of life and death. You find yourself asking, "Why us? Why now? Why this?" You question everything you once took for granted, seeking answers that often don't come. For some, faith becomes a source of strength and comfort, a lifeline in the midst of the storm. For others, it becomes a struggle, a wrestling with God in search of meaning and purpose amidst the pain.

But amidst the darkness, there are also moments of light—moments of profound love, connection, and grace. You see the strength of the human spirit in ways you never thought possible. You witness the power of community as friends, family, and even strangers come together to offer support, prayers, and acts of kindness. You learn to appreciate the small things—the laughter of a child, the beauty of a sunset, the comfort of a warm embrace. You find strength you didn't know you had, and you discover the depth of love that can sustain you through even the darkest of times.

Cancer is a journey, one that no one chooses but one that many are forced to walk. It's a journey marked by pain, loss, and uncertainty, but also by courage, resilience, and hope. It destroys, yes, but it also reveals. It reveals the strength of the human spirit, the power of love, and the importance of cherishing every moment.

As I reflect on my own journey with cancer, I am reminded of the preciousness of life, the importance of family, and the enduring power of hope. Yes, cancer destroys, but it does not define us. It does not have the final word. In the midst of the storm, we find ways to rebuild, to heal, and to live again. We find ways to honor the memories of those we've lost and to cherish the time we have with those we love. We find ways to keep moving forward, one step at a time, trusting that there is still light ahead, even in the darkest of nights.

So, to anyone who is walking this path, know that you are not alone. Know that your pain is valid, your tears are seen, and your strength is acknowledged. Know that there is hope, even in the midst of despair. And know that we are all in this together, fighting, praying, and believing for a better tomorrow.

CHAPTER 14
LIFE AFTER LOSS: A WIDOW'S JOURNEY

It has been ten years since I lost Elijah, my beloved husband of forty-one years, yet it feels as if it happened just yesterday. The grief still sits heavy in my heart, a constant companion that I've had to learn to live with. Each day has been a journey, a battle to find my footing in a world that feels so unfamiliar without him by my side. The life we built together, once filled with love, laughter, and shared dreams, now feels like a distant memory. I am left to navigate this new reality as a widow, a title I never thought I'd have to bear.

In the beginning, the loneliness was overwhelming. I remember waking up each morning, reaching out instinctively to his side of the bed, only to find it cold and empty. The emptiness of our home was a stark reminder of his absence. The silence was deafening; every creak of the floorboards and every tick of the clock echoed through the hollow rooms like a painful reminder of the life that was no longer there. The mornings were the hardest. I would wake up, and for a fleeting moment, I would forget. Then, like a cruel trick, reality would come crashing down. Elijah was gone, and I was alone.

The days that followed his passing felt like a blur. I was surrounded by friends and family who came to offer their support, but their presence only served to amplify the void that Elijah had left behind. People would say, "I'm so sorry for your loss," or "He's in a better place now," but none of those words could penetrate the numbness that enveloped me. I was grateful for their kindness, but I longed for something they couldn't give me: I longed for Elijah.

Grief is a strange and unpredictable thing. It comes in waves, sometimes gentle, lapping at your feet, other times like a tidal wave, threatening to pull you under. There were moments when I would find myself crying without warning, the tears spilling over at the sight of his favorite chair, a song on the radio, or the scent of his cologne lingering on his clothes. At other times, I would feel nothing at all, as if my heart had gone numb from the pain. The weight of the sorrow was suffocating, and I struggled to find a way to breathe again.

Friends and family encouraged me to "move on" or "find a new normal," but what did that even mean? How does one "move on" from a loss so profound, from a life built over decades, only to have it all taken away in an instant? The idea of moving on felt like a betrayal, like I was somehow dishonoring Elijah's memory. I didn't want to move on; I wanted to hold on—to the memories, to the life we shared, to him.

As the months went by, I realized that grief does not have a timeline. It does not follow a neat, orderly path. It's messy and unpredictable, and it changes you. I began to understand that I wasn't the same person I was before Elijah died. I was a widow now, and that came with its own set of challenges. Simple things that I had never thought about before—like going to the grocery store or attending church services—became daunting tasks. Everywhere I went, I was reminded of what I had lost. I would see couples holding hands or hear someone laughing, and I would be reminded of how much I missed him. The loneliness was a constant ache, a hollow feeling that settled deep in my bones.

But amidst the sorrow, I began to find moments of peace. I started taking long walks in the mornings, finding solace in the quiet of nature. The birdsong, the rustling leaves, and the gentle warmth of the sun on my face became small comforts in a world that felt so dark. I began to journal, writing down my thoughts and feelings, pouring my grief onto the pages. It was a way to release the emotions I had been holding in, a way to connect with Elijah in a different way. I wrote him letters, telling him about my day, my fears, and my hopes. It was a way to keep him close, to feel like he was still a part of my life.

I also found comfort in my faith. I prayed a lot during those days—sometimes in anger, sometimes in despair, but mostly for strength. I needed strength to get through each day, to face a future that seemed so uncertain without Elijah. My faith became a lifeline, a source of hope in a time of deep despair. I began attending a grief support group. It was there that I met others who were going through the same pain, who understood the unique challenges of being a widow. We shared our stories, our tears, and in those moments of shared sorrow, I found a sense of community, a reminder that I was not alone.

Gradually, I started to rebuild my life. I learned to take things one day at a time, to find joy in the small, simple moments. I rekindled old hobbies—gardening, reading, writing,—finding comfort in the familiar routines. Slowly but surely, I began to carve out a new existence for myself, one that honored Elijah's memory but also allowed me to live again.

There were setbacks, of course. There were days when the grief would hit me all over again, like a wound freshly opened. But I learned to be gentle with myself, to give myself grace. I learned that it was okay to feel sadness, to miss him, and to cry. I also learned that it was okay to smile, to laugh, to find happiness again. Being a widow meant learning to hold both joy and sorrow in the same breath, to live with the duality of grief and gratitude.

I am still learning, still navigating this new chapter of my life without Elijah. I know that the pain of his loss will never fully go away, but I am learning to carry it with me, to let it be a part of my story without letting it define me. I am learning that life, even after such a profound loss, can still hold beauty and meaning. And I am learning that while Elijah may no longer be with me in the physical sense, his spirit, his love, will always be a part of me, guiding me through this journey of widowhood, reminding me that I am never truly alone.

Life after loss is a journey, one filled with ups and downs, with moments of despair and moments of hope. It is a journey I did not choose, but one I must walk. And as I continue to put one foot in front of the other, I do so with the knowledge that I carry Elijah with me in my heart, in my memories, in every step I take.

CHAPTER 15
IF I COULD TURN BACK THE HANDS OF TIME

If I could turn back the hands of time, there are so many moments I would revisit. Not to change them, but to savor them. To hold onto the joy, the laughter, the innocence of a life untouched by the cruel hands of cancer. I often think about life before the diagnosis, before our world was turned upside down, and I wonder what our story would have been like if cancer had never entered it. What if we had been allowed to live out our days as we always dreamed—growing old together, holding hands through the years, and watching our love mature with the passing of time?

I find myself thinking back to the day we got married. I can still see it so clearly, as if it happened just yesterday. Elijah, standing there, looking so handsome and full of life, waiting for me at the altar. And me, nervous but excited, ready to start this new chapter of our lives together. When we exchanged our vows, we promised to love each other in sickness and in health, but back then, we couldn't have imagined what that would really mean. We were young and full of dreams. We talked about the future as if it were guaranteed. We imagined ourselves growing old together, sitting on our front porch in rocking chairs, reminiscing about the good old days.

Those early years of our marriage were full of promise. We were building a life together, learning how to navigate the challenges of adulthood, and all the while, our love was growing stronger. We didn't have much in terms of material things, but we had each other, and that was more than enough. We dreamed of the family we would build, the home we would create, and the life we would live. We didn't know what the future held, but we were confident that as long as we had each other, we could face anything.

If I could turn back the hands of time, I'd return to those simpler days. I'd go back to our first apartment, the one with the leaky faucet, the tiny kitchen and the sunken living room that I loved. We didn't care about the little inconveniences; we were too busy building a life, dreaming of the future, and laughing at the silly things we did to make ends meet. I'd return to the nights we stayed up late, talking about our dreams, planning our future, and promising to be each other's forever. We were so sure that we'd have all the time in the world.

But life has a way of surprising you. Time, it seems, is never as plentiful as we think it is. When cancer entered our lives, it felt like someone had pressed pause on the life we had envisioned. All the plans, the dreams, and the hopes we had for our future were suddenly overshadowed by doctor's appointments, treatments, and endless waiting rooms. The carefree days we once enjoyed were replaced with uncertainty, fear, and the overwhelming weight of illness. But through it all, we held onto each other, just like we promised we would. In sickness and in health, we remained side by side.

Still, I often wonder what it would have been like if cancer hadn't stolen those years from us. I imagine us living out the life we had planned, free from the shadow of illness. I think about the trips never taken, Europe, the cruise to Alaska, the milestones we would have celebrated, and the quiet, peaceful moments we would have shared. If I could turn back the hands of time, I'd take us to a place where cancer didn't exist, where our days were filled with the simple joys of being together.

We had always dreamed of growing old together. We talked about what it would be like to watch our children grow up, to see them get married and start families of their own. Thank You Father that Elijah was able to see our sons grown, married with children. And our daughter with a career she loves.

We looked forward to the day when it would just be the two of us again, sitting in our cozy home, reflecting on all we had built together. We would have celebrated our golden years, a testament to the love that had carried us through the ups and downs of life.

If I could turn back the hands of time, I'd hold onto those moments when we were just starting out, full of excitement for the life we were building. I'd savor the days when our biggest worries were small, when our love was the center of our world, and when the future seemed so bright and full of possibilities. I'd remind myself to cherish the little things—the way Elijah would make me laugh, the way he would hold me close when I was feeling unsure, and the way we'd dream together about a life that stretched far into the future.

But the truth is, time marches on, whether we are ready or not. And while we couldn't stop the events that unfolded, I find comfort in knowing that we lived our life with love, even through the hardest moments. I would not trade our time together for anything, not even the parts where cancer tried to break us. Because through it all, our love remained strong. And even though we did not get the future we had hoped for, we had each other, and that was enough.

If I could turn back the hands of time, I wouldn't change our story, but I would take more time to appreciate the moments we had. I would hold onto each day a little tighter, laugh a little longer, and love with an even greater intensity. Because now I know how precious those moments were. I know that life is fragile, and time is a gift we must never take for granted.

We may not have had the life we dreamed of when we first got married, but we lived our lives together with a love that was deep and true. And in the end, that's what matters most. Cancer may have taken Elijah from me, but it can never take away the love we shared or the memories we created. If I could bring back the hands of time, I'd do it all again, because loving Elijah has been the greatest gift of my life.

CHAPTER 16
SEE YOU LATER, NOT GOODBYE

In our family, "goodbye" was a word that held too much weight, too much finality. It was a word we avoided instinctively, replacing it with something softer, more hopeful: "See you later." Those three simple words carried the promise of reunion, a reminder that parting was never permanent. Whether we were leaving the house for a quick trip to the store, heading off to school, or ending a phone call, we would always say, "See you later." It became more than just a habit; it was a thread that held us together, a mantra that reassured us of our enduring connection.

Elijah was the first to insist on it. He had a way of making even the smallest interactions meaningful. Every morning before leaving for work, he would lean down, kiss me on the forehead, and say, "See you later." He'd then turn to our children, adding his trademark grin, and repeat, "See you later, kiddos. Be good for your mom!" Even when life got busy, and the words were hurried, they were never forgotten. It was his way of reminding us that, no matter how far apart we might be, we were always tethered to one another by love.

I vividly remember one summer evening when Elijah explained why he never said "goodbye." We were sitting in our backyard, watching the sun dip below the horizon. "Goodbye feels too final," he said, his voice steady and sure. "It's like saying you'll never see someone again. But 'See you later'? That's different. It's a promise. It means, 'I'll be back, and so will you.'" That night, his words sank deep into my heart, shaping how I viewed the people I loved and the moments we shared.

Even as our children grew older, moved out, and started families of their own, "See you later" remained a constant. It was the last thing we said to each other during family gatherings, no matter how late the hour. I remember Allen teasing Elijah once, saying, "Dad, you'd say 'See you later' even if I were moving to the moon." Elijah just laughed and replied, "That's right, son. And I'd find a way to get there, too."

When Elijah passed away, the weight of his absence was overwhelming. For the first time, I struggled to hold on to the tradition he had instilled in us. How could I say "See you later" when he wouldn't be walking through the door anymore? The house felt emptier without his laughter, without the reassuring presence that had always filled every corner. I missed the sound of him saying those words to me, that quiet promise that we would always be together.

In the days and weeks after his passing, I found myself clinging to the memories we had shared.

As time has passed, I've come to realize that Elijah was right all along. "See you later" isn't just a phrase— it's a promise, a declaration of faith that love transcends time and space. It's a reminder that our bonds don't end when someone leaves this world. Instead, they live on, carried in our hearts and memories, until the day we're reunited.

And so, to my beloved Elijah: even though you are no longer here with us, this is not goodbye. It never will be. It's "See you later." One day, in God's perfect time, I will see you again, and we'll pick up right where we left off, just as we always promised.

Until then, my love, see you later.

CHAPTER 17
HOLDING YOU CLOSE IN MY HEART:
A LETTER TO ELIJAH

Dear Elijah,

It's been a while since I last wrote to you, and I find myself missing you more with each passing day. Even though you are no longer physically here, I still feel your presence around me in so many ways. Writing to you helps me feel close to you, as if I could still share my day and my thoughts with you, like we used to. There are so many things I wish I could tell you, so many moments I wish I could share with you.

Today was one of those days where I felt the weight of your absence more than usual. I went through my day trying to keep busy—running errands, tidying up around the house, and catching up with some friends from church. But no matter how much I do, there's always this empty space, a silence that feels louder than anything else. I miss the way we used to talk about everything and nothing. I miss the comfort of your voice, the warmth of your presence, and the way you always knew how to make me feel safe, no matter what was going on.

I've been feeling a lot of fears lately. I worry about what the future holds without you here by my side. I wonder how I'll navigate the rest of my life on my own, without your guidance and your love to light my path. I'm scared of the loneliness that sometimes feels overwhelming, of the nights that seem too long, and the days that seem to drag on without your laughter to brighten them. I worry about whether I'm strong enough to keep going, to keep finding joy and purpose without you here to share it with me.

But even in the midst of these fears, I find hope. I find hope in the memories we created together the love we shared, and the life we built. I hold on to the hope that you are still watching over me, guiding me from above, just as you did when you were here. I hope that I can continue to make you proud, to live a life that honors the love we had and the dreams we dreamed together.

I've also been thinking a lot about our family. I worry about the kids and how they're handling things. I see pieces of you in each of them—the way they laugh, the way they love, and even in their stubborn determination. They miss you too, more than words can say. I try to be strong for them, to be the rock that you always were, but some days are harder than others. I hope they know how much you loved them and that you are still with them in spirit, guiding them and watching over them.

You know, Elijah, I've been trying to find new ways to keep myself busy and to keep my mind occupied. I've taken up some new hobbies—things I thought might bring me some peace or at least a distraction. I've started gardening again. I remember how much you loved the garden, how you would spend hours out there, tending to the flowers and the vegetables. I can almost hear your voice, giving me tips on how to make the roses bloom just right or how to keep the weeds from taking over. It brings me a sense of comfort, being out there among the flowers, feeling like a part of you is still with me, still guiding my hands.

I've also been leaning heavily on my faith, Elijah. You always taught me the importance of trusting in God's plan, even when we don't understand it. Some days, that trust is all that keeps me going. I pray every day for the strength to face this new chapter of my life without you, to find joy and purpose even in the midst of my sorrow. I pray that God gives me the courage to face my fears and the grace to embrace the future with hope, knowing that you would want me to keep living, to keep loving, and to keep finding happiness.

Sometimes, I find myself talking to you, asking you for advice, as if you could still answer me. I ask you what you think I should do about this or that, or how you would handle a particular situation. It's strange, but it brings me comfort, imagining what you would say, hearing your voice in my mind. I guess it's my way of keeping you close, of not letting go of the connection we shared.

I know you would want me to be happy, to find peace, and to live my life to the fullest. I'm trying, Elijah, I really am. I'm trying to find joy in the little things, to be grateful for the blessings I still have, and to trust that there is still a purpose for me here. I hope you know how much I love you, how much I miss you, and how much I wish you were still here with me. But I also hope you know that I am doing my best to honor your memory, to live a life that reflects the love and joy we shared.

So, until I see you again, I will keep writing to you, keep talking to you, and keep carrying you with me in my heart. Thank you for being the love of my life, for giving me so many beautiful memories, and for showing me what it means to truly love and be loved. I will hold onto that love for the rest of my days.

With all my love,

Carolyn

CHAPTER 18
A VALENTINE FROM HEAVEN

February 14, 2023—Valentine's Day. The air was crisp with a hint of lingering winter, but the sun cast a warm glow through the bedroom windows. I decided to spend the afternoon cleaning out one of the bedrooms, a task I'd been putting off for months. As I sorted through old boxes and dust-covered shelves, I stumbled upon a stack of forgotten papers tied together with a faded ribbon.

Curiosity piqued, I sat on the edge of the bed and began to sift through the assortment of memories: old letters, photographs, and miscellaneous notes. Among them, a particular envelope caught my eye. It was adorned with delicate hearts and bore my name in Elijah's unmistakable handwriting. My heart skipped a beat.

Gently opening the envelope, I pulled out a Valentine's Day card. The card was simple yet elegant, With the words TOGETHER written on the front. Inside it was about us and how we had supported each other through the years and how together we had grown so much in love,

The Valentines Day Card
From Elijah from 1997

A wave of emotions washed over me. I couldn't recall which year he had given me this card, but it didn't matter. At that moment, it felt as if Elijah was reaching out to me from beyond, reminding me of the eternal bond we share. Tears welled up in my eyes, not of sorrow, but of profound love and gratitude.

Just then, I heard the front door open. My son Allen had come to visit. Wiping away my tears, I hurried downstairs, clutching the card to my chest.

"Mom, are you okay?" Allen asked, noticing my flushed face.

"Allen, you won't believe what I just found," I exclaimed, my voice trembling with excitement. "I found a valentine card your father had given me years ago today—as if it was from heaven!"

He looked at me puzzled. "What do you mean?"

I handed him the card. As he read through it, a soft smile formed on his face. "Mom, this is incredible."

"I know," I said softly. "It's like he's still here with us, reminding me of his love."

Allen chuckled warmly. "You know, I brought you candy and flowers today," he said, gesturing to the gifts he'd placed on the kitchen counter. "But it seems Dad, even in death, won't let another man—even his own son—outdo him."

We both laughed, the sound filling the house with a joy that had been absent for too long. It was as if Elijah's presence was woven into that very moment, bridging the gap between past and present.

"He's always had impeccable timing," I mused.

Allen nodded. "Dad wouldn't have it any other way."

The Flowers and Cake from Allen, my son and the Card found that Valentines Day from Elijah.

We spent the rest of the afternoon reminiscing about Elijah—his quirks, his laughter, the way he could light up a room just by being in it. The house felt alive again, filled with stories and the palpable essence of a love that transcends time and space.

As the sun began to set, casting hues of pink and orange across the sky, I realized that Valentine's Day had brought me an unexpected gift. Not just the rediscovered card, but the reminder that love endures, living on in our hearts and memories. Elijah's love was still here, guiding me, comforting me, and yes, even playfully competing with our son.

That night, I placed the card on my bedside table. It served as a beautiful testament to the life we shared and the unbreakable bond that continues to connect us. I fell asleep with a peaceful heart, grateful for the love that had touched my life so profoundly.

The next morning, I awoke with a renewed sense of hope. I decided to frame the card, so it could serve as a daily reminder of Elijah's enduring love. Life moves forward, but some connections remain unbroken, echoing through the corridors of time.

And so, Valentine's Day became not just a celebration of love, but a celebration of life, memories, and the unseen threads that bind us to those we've loved and lost. It's comforting to know that sometimes, love finds a way to reach us—even from heaven.

EPILOGUE

As I sit and reflect on the journey Elijah and I shared, I am struck by the beauty of a life built on love, faith, and unwavering commitment. Though the years we had together were far too brief, they were filled with moments that will live forever in my heart. The laughter, the struggles, the triumphs, and the quiet evenings when words were not necessary—all of it shaped the tapestry of a life deeply lived.

Elijah's love continues to guide me, even in his absence. I feel his presence in the small things: the warmth of the morning sun, the scent of his favorite cologne lingering in the memories of our home, and the laughter of our family as we share stories about him. His legacy is not confined to the years he walked this earth; it lives on in every life he touched, every act of kindness he offered, and the strength he showed in the face of trials.

Writing this book has been a journey of its own— a way to honor Elijah and the life we built together. It allowed me to revisit the precious memories and, in doing so, realize that love is eternal. Though he is no longer here with me physically, his love is woven into the fabric of my soul, giving me strength to face each day.

I hope this story inspires others to cherish their loved ones, to hold fast to hope even in the darkest moments, and to never take for granted the bonds that make life so meaningful. Life is fleeting, but love endures forever.

To Elijah, my beloved husband: the love we had stays on my mind and forever in my heart. Thank you for showing me what true love looks like. Until we meet again.

Elijah and Family 1983

ABOUT THE AUTHOR

Dr. Carolyn Brown is an accomplished author, playwright director, with her plays having been performed in New York and Virginia. She worked for over 20 years as an economic assistant with the Department of Labor, contributing to the Consumer Price Index. Dr. Brown holds a Bachelor's Degree in Religious Education, a Master's in Christian Education, and a Doctorate in Christian Ministry. She attended Norfolk State College (now Norfolk State University) in Norfolk, Virginia, Queens College in Queens, New York, and All Christian Bible College in Deer Park, New York. She was 'married to her late husband, Elijah, for forty-one years and is the mother of three children, grandmother of nine, and great-grandmother of seven.

Currently, Dr. Brown serves as an associate minister at New Covenant Church of Christ (Baptist) in Queens Village, New York.

As an author, her first book, The Perfect Relationship (How Imperfect People Can Create the Perfect Relationship), was published in 2018, and she is preparing to release her third book by early 2025.

THE PERFECT RELATIONSHIP
BY CAROLYN BROWN

In "The Perfect Relationship," nine friends—Claudia, Quiana, Camille, Carol, Kima, Briana, Melody, Marjorie, and Kayla—unite in their quest to find true love and build lasting marriages. Deeply believing in love and guided by their faith, each woman prays to God for the wisdom to choose the right husband before entering marriage. However, like many couples, they encounter numerous challenges that test their relationships, from misunderstandings and unmet expectations to betrayal and heartbreak.

As these women navigate the ups and downs of married life, the book explores how they cope with everyday stresses and significant trials. Their stories highlight whether their resilience and faith can sustain their relationships or lead to their unraveling. Despite their hopes and careful choices, many discover that the men they believed would bring them happiness ultimately fall short, leaving the women to grapple with disappointment and betrayal.

"The Perfect Relationship" is a poignant reflection on love, faith, and the strength of female friendship, illustrating that true perfection in relationships comes from overcoming challenges.

FOR BOOKINGS AND ORDERS:

To order bulk copies of *The Love We Had Stays on My Mind* or to book Dr. Carolyn Brown for speaking engagements, book signings, or interviews, please contact:

Website: www.DrCarolynBrown.com
Email: Carolyn@DrCarolynBrown.com
Phone: 646-610-1140